HISTORY IN CAMERA

CANALS AND WATERWAYS

Michael E. Ware

Shire Publications Ltd

Set in 11 point Times roman and printed in Great Britain by C. I. Thomas & Sons (Haverfordwest) Ltd, Press Buildings, Merlins Bridge, Haverfordwest, Dyfed.

British Library Cataloguing in Publication Data available.

Front cover: *This 1905 scene is the Widcombe flight of locks in Bath on the Kennet and Avon Canal. This canal linked with the river Thames to give a through route from London to Bristol, completed in 1810. John Rennie was the engineer in charge. His canal was 57 miles (92 km) long, had 79 locks and could take boats up to 73 feet (22 metres) long and 13 feet 10 inches (4.2 metres) wide. This is a contemporary black and white photograph which has been expertly coloured, making it into a most attractive picture postcard. Postcard photographers often gathered groups of children together to add human interest to a scene.*

Contents

Title page: *A winter scene on the Trent and Mersey Canal at Whatcroft, near Northwich, in the 1930s.*

Below: *Boats at Newton Locks on the Leeds and Liverpool Canal, about 1905.*

1. *The first artificial waterway in Britain was the Fossdyke dug by the Romans from the Trent to Lincoln. After the Romans left it fell into disuse and when in the eighteenth century plans were made to improve the navigation there was the usual clash between those with drainage interests and those who wished to keep the water levels up for navigation. Here, in 1930, a keel is seen under sail at Saxilby on the Fossdyke; having just negotiated the swing-bridge, it is getting under way again.*

1. Canal mania

It was the Romans who built the first artificial waterways in Britain, one of which was the Fossdyke linking the river Trent with the river Witham near Lincoln. The Romans also built a network of good roads to serve the needs of their armies. When the Romans left, there was no central government capable of looking after such things and both the waterways and the roads fell into disrepair.

At the start of the industrial revolution in the mid eighteenth century road transport was poor. Tracks which were baked hard in the summer would be a quagmire in the winter. They were not suitable for carrying the heavy and bulky goods needed for or made by the newly emerging industries. Some rivers had been dredged and made navigable by means of flash locks but there were not always rivers where the goods were required. The coming of the pound lock in 1577 on the river Lee helped to make river navigation more efficient. The first true artificial waterway in eighteenth-century England was the 8 mile (13 km) St Helens Canal, which made the Sankey Brook navigable down to the river Mersey. Opened in 1757, it was physically separated from the Sankey Brook itself and so it ought to be acknowledged as the first canal, although the distinction is usually given to the Bridgewater Canal running from the Duke of Bridgewater's estates at Worsley outside Manchester into the city itself, a distance of 10½ miles (17 km).

The Duke of Bridgewater had realised that he needed to get coal from his mines to a much wider range of customers, and the only way to do this was to improve its transport. James Gilbert, the Duke's estate agent, was entrusted with the job of overseeing this canal project. It was Gilbert who introduced the Duke to a millwright named James Brindley, who had a reputation as an ingenious engineer. An Act of Parliament authorising the scheme was passed in 1759 and the Duke just succeeded in raising enough money for the project, which is thought to be the only major canal that was financed by one person. The canal was completed in 1761. Much of the water for the canal was drainage water from the coal mines and later the drainage tunnels were converted to underground canals so that it eventually became possible to load a canal boat at the coal seam itself. Originally the Manchester terminus was at the bottom of Castle Hill, so the customers had a difficult journey with their heavy loads. Later the canal was run into the hill itself, a vertical shaft was sunk from above and the coal was pulled to the top of the hill by crane, powered by a waterwheel. The loads of coal were placed in large boxes (the equivalent of the modern containers) at the coal face so it was easy to lift these up the shaft. The principal engineering work on the canal was an aqueduct at Barton over the river Irwell. It was 200 yards (180 metres) long and 39 feet (12 metres) above the level of the river.

With the coming of the canal to Manchester, the cost of coal in the city dropped by almost half. Canals were to have the same effect elsewhere in England and Wales. Whilst still working on the Bridgewater Canal and its later extension to Runcorn to join the Mersey via a staircase of barge-size locks, Brindley was approached to become the engineer for a projected canal to join the Trent with the Mersey. One of the promoters was Josiah

2. *From earliest times man has tried to make rivers navigable. One of the problems facing these early river engineers was that of shifting shoals and dredging. The spoon dredger was crude and primitive but was still in regular use during the nineteenth century, and on some canals well into the twentieth century. Here a team of three spoon dredgers is seen on the upper reaches of the Thames in 1900. The scoop spooned the mud from the bed of the navigation and placed it in the dredging punt.*

Canal mania

3. The home of the inland canal system — Worsley, some 10½ miles (17 km) from Manchester. The coal mines belonging to Francis, Duke of Bridgewater, are a short distance up a branch to the right of the attractive packet house. From the steps of this house passenger packet boats used to run to Manchester. Loaded and unloaded narrowboats are seen in this 1908 photograph along with a wider-beam craft.

4. Coal at Worsley was at first mined in the conventional manner from above. Drainage tunnels were dug to take away surplus water and later these were made navigable. These are some of the special mine boats or 'starvationers' used within the mine and even on the Bridgewater Canal. This photograph was taken soon after the closure of the mines in 1887.

5 (above). *Almost from the first days of the Bridgewater Canal coal was carried in containers. This rare photograph of the box boats was taken early in the twentieth century at Astley Green Colliery, just a few miles from Worsley. Each container held 35 cwt of coal. Other versions had opening doors at the bottom.*

6 (opposite, top). *The expanding pottery industry had pressed for a canal passing through the Six Towns of the Potteries. Here at Fenton Dock, Runcorn, the coastal craft are seen bringing in the raw materials, some of which are being transferred to the diminutive narrowboats. The crated crockery for export was stored in the warehouses in the background.*

7 (opposite, bottom). *The art of roadmaking was only just being learned when the Trent and Mersey Canal was built. For many years still, however, it was difficult to move heavy loads in winter: ten horses might be required to move a cart carrying a ton or so of goods, so this narrowboat, photographed at Whatcroft near Northwich in the 1930s with 25 tons of felspar, replaces a great many horse and carts (or packhorses). This was the importance of the coming of canals.*

Wedgwood, whose pottery at Etruria near Stoke-on-Trent required clay from Devon and Cornwall. This was brought up the river Weaver and then onward by packhorse. Finished crocks were also carried by packhorse and contemporary reports tell us that a high percentage was broken. The Trent and Mersey Canal was different in character to the original lockless line of the Bridgewater. It had 76 locks and its largest engineering feature was the 2897 yard (2649 metre) Harecastle Tunnel. Brindley died before the Trent and Mersey was completed in 1777. Later this

8. (above). *One of the greatest engineering feats of its day was the Barton Aqueduct, which carried the Bridgewater Canal over the navigable river Irwell. The famous engineer Smeaton, when he saw the plans of the project, is reputed to have said: 'I have heard of castles in the air, but never before have I seen where any of them were to be erected.' This is a rare photograph of the aqueduct taken before it was demolished in 1890 to make way for the Manchester Ship Canal. Note the pollution in the river.*

9 (opposite, top). *The Harecastle Tunnel was the first major canal tunnel in Britain. It was, however, built to such a small bore that by 1827 a parallel tunnel had to be built to eliminate one-way working by timetable. James Brindley's original tunnel was later closed because of mining subsidence, which has also caused the damage to the bridge parapet in this photograph taken around 1939.*

10 (opposite, bottom). *The earliest form of lock to be found on navigable rivers was the flash lock or watergate. A single gate in a weir holds back the water. When a boat wishes to pass above the weir the watergate is winched back and the boat flows through. A boat coming upstream has to be winched against the current through the gap in the weir. One of the last of such flash locks was Cropthorne Watergate on the Warwickshire Avon, photographed here in the 1940s. The derelict gate is open, but the equipement for winding it back against the head of water is clearly seen.*

canal was linked with the Thames at Oxford and the Severn at Stourport, to form a great cross-shaped system of canals through the Midlands.

It was not difficult to see the advantages of canal communication, mainly for the carriage of goods, although some passengers were carried. Canal mania set in. Every town and village seemed to want a canal. It was said that by 1800 'there was nowhere south of Durham more than 15 miles from water communication', although this was an exaggeration. Many canals were planned and many were built, many others were not, while some were started but never finished. Some people made a lot of money;

others lost a lot. Some canal shares are reputed to have increased in value by thirty times.

Canal mania can be said to have ended with the building of the Birmingham and Liverpool Junction Canal (now the Shropshire Union) by Thomas Telford in 1835. By this time it was realised that canals were coming into direct competition with the newfangled railways. Indeed, the first railway locomotive was tested on a tramway that led down to the Glamorganshire Canal. Brindley had warned that canals would be threatened by 'tramroads' but it happened earlier than he had expected. Throughout the nineteenth century the two forms of transport operated side by side. In some cases railways took over canal companies. Whether in private or railway ownership, many canals closed because of the railway competition.

11. *In the Churnet Valley the railway and the canal run side by side. In hilly areas it was not unusual to find the railway close to the canal, for the canal engineers had often found the easiest route. Like the canals, the railways had the problem that unless goods could be loaded into the trucks at the commencement of the journey and straight into the receiver's premises at the end of the journey transhipment and road haulage were necessary. As the roads improved so road haulage all the way became a more attractive proposition.*

2. The canal and its structures

Once a canal had been promoted, it required an Act of Parliament. The Act would contain many clauses, amongst which would be those dealing with the raising of capital by the issuing of shares. They would stipulate the tolls to be charged and compensation to be paid to landowners, the power to divert streams and so on. Even the steepness of the gradients leading up to bridges could be specified. Hump-back bridges over canals are often a legacy of an original Canal Act. Money had to be raised. Snags often arose in construction and money tended to run out, necessitating a second share issue. The chief engineer of a canal, a man such as James Brindley, William Jessop, Benjamin Outram or John Rennie, would often be working on a number of different projects at one time, and so a resident engineer was employed to be on site at the canal from day to day. During the building of these canals there were no mechanical aids available to the engineers. Everything was done by hand by navigators, or 'navvies', as they became better known. At first these workers were drawn locally from the area through which the canal was passing. With so many canals being built, even men with slight skills were in demand, so navvies tended to join forces into gangs under a foreman or contractor and move from job to job.

Water engineering was not a new profession where it applied to rivers, but artificial waterways had problems of their own. Unlike rivers, they had to be made watertight. Water supply on a canal was often scarce, especially where it crossed a high plateau. Brindley developed the idea of 'puddling'. A layer of clay was laid on the base and the sides of the canal, then mixed with a little water and kneaded to a substance which remained remarkably watertight. Often the puddling was achieved by driving a herd of cows along the bed of the new waterway.

The dimensions of the Bridgewater Canal were such that the local craft (Mersey flats) could trade on it, and the flight of locks built later at Runcorn, for example, were 14 feet (4.3 metres) wide to take these craft. Once Brindley began working on the major cross-country canals he saw the need to build them to a smaller dimension. He built his locks 7 feet (2.1 metres) wide and 72 feet (22 metres) long. By setting this size for the lock, he dictated the maximum size for a boat. He also set the maximum dimensions for each bridge hole and the tunnels. It is the locks which make a canal such a versatile form of transport. They allow

the waterways to go either uphill or downhill. Admittedly each lock was a hold-up for a passing boat, but in those days time was not worth so much money as it is today.

A pound lock is a brick-lined chamber (occasionally it was turf-lined on river navigations) with swinging doors or gates at each end. The top gate on a narrow canal is usually a single gate, whilst at the bottom two gates are mitred to fit together in a shallow V, using the force of the water in the lock to hold them shut. Water is let into the lock by means of sluices known as

12 (opposite, top). *For nearly 150 years navvies played a very important part in the social and economic history of Britain. They arrived when the first canals were being built, and when canal mania had passed they moved on to build the railways. This group were some of the last to be employed on a waterway project (the Manchester Ship Canal in 1887). At one time over 1700 were employed building this inland trade route.*

13 (opposite, bottom). *The canals were built entirely by hand, with horses and carts being used to carry spoil away from the site. Spades and wheelbarrows were the standard tools. This photograph is of repair rather than building, and even though it was taken as late as October 1942 it shows all the traditional methods, particularly the wheelbarrow run. It is the Shropshire Union Canal at Nantwich.*

14 (below). *Canals had to be watertight. The commonest method of ensuring this was to line the bed with a thick layer of clay. In this photograph workmen are digging clay by hand for this purpose in 1904. Conveniently, the source of clay at Blue House Reach on the Thames and Severn Canal was very close to the line of the canal. Often it had to be transported many miles, either by horse and cart or on part of the newly built waterway.*

15 (above). *During major repairs on the Thames and Severn Canal in the early twentieth century long stretches of the canal were rebuilt. One of the principal problems of this canal had always been leakage. This gang of workmen are 'puddling' a new clay lining. This stretch of canal at Puck Mill lower lock was reputed to 'empty itself about every four hours'. Though it was not so important on river navigations, artificial canals had to be watertight. A canal could not afford to lose water or cause flooding.*

16 (opposite). *By setting the size for the lock, James Brindley dictated the maximum size for a boat. This is beautifully illustrated in this photograph taken by Fred H. Done on the Audlem flight of locks on the Shropshire Union Canal in the 1930s. A pair of fully loaded boats approaches a narrow lock and, as can be seen, there is very little room to spare. The average rise on a lock such as this would be 6 feet (1.8 metres).*

paddles, either around the gates through underground channels or on the gates themselves. When the water level in a lock is equivalent to that on the outside, little effort is required to push on the lock-gate beam to open the gates.

A canal is a running stream, albeit a slow-moving one, with water coming in at the highest point and leaving at the lowest. Therefore there must be a bypass at each lock, and this usually takes the form of a by-pass weir and channel alongside. Most of the narrow locks on the English canal system have a fall of 6 feet (1.8 metres) or so. The deepest is, however, 14 feet (4.3 metres). Where a canal is engineered up a relatively steep piece of ground, the locks are grouped together and called a 'flight'. If the ground is steeper still, the flight is sometimes engineered as a staircase. In this case, one lock leads directly into the next. The most impressive staircase in England is at Bingley, West Yorkshire, on the broad Leeds and Liverpool Canal, with five locks each opening directly into the next one.

17. *Pound locks all work in the same way. This is a wide lock on the Grand Junction Canal. Locks are usually built of brick, including the bottom. The paddle holes which allow the water to empty are just visible on the new lock gates. An average wide lock would hold 50,000 gallons (227,000 litres) of water. The workmen are draining the seepage with single wooden scoops or scopes.*

18. *Many of the locks on the Grand Union Canal were fitted with four gate paddles as well as two ground paddles. The ground paddles were opened first, and when the lock was half full the gate paddles could be opened, allowing the lock to fill very quickly. The gate paddles had to be used with caution as premature opening could flood the boats. All paddles are open on this Second World War photograph of a lock on the Stoke Bruerne flight.*

19. *A rare type of lock on the canal system is the guillotine lock. Most examples are to be found on the canalised rivers, such as the Nene. This is a rare photograph of the guillotine lock at Lifford Lane on the Stratford-on-Avon Canal in use in the 1920s. This lock went out of use in 1928 but is kept intact as a museum piece. The boat is a Birmingham day boat, a craft on which the rudder could be fixed at either end. Here it is proceeding cabin first.*

A canal needs a source of water at its highest point. This could be in the form of a stream or lake, or more likely an artificial reservoir. Where water is not available at the highest level it has to be pumped there from a supply lower down. The summit level of the Kennet and Avon Canal at Crofton is a good example of this. Here two great steam beam engines, now restored by enthusiasts, pump water from Wilton Water (the reservoir) up 40 feet (12 metres) to the summit level. It was essential that the water source was constant throughout the year and that it should not dry out in the summers.

Where it was necessary for a canal to cross a valley an aqueduct was often built. Although the Romans built the first aqueducts, these were to carry water supplies rather than navigable waterways. One of the principal problems with an aqueduct was its bulk as it had to support a watertight canal usually lined with

20. *This unusual view shows the staircase of locks, one chamber leading into the next, on the Shropshire Union Canal at Chester. On this occasion the locks had been emptied for repairs. It can be clearly seen that the lock gate fits flush against the sill, making it watertight. Its effectiveness can be seen on the top gates, which are holding back a mile-long pound of water, but little of it is leaking past.*

21. *The best known example of a staircase of locks on a wide canal (14 feet, 4.3 metres) occurs at Bingley on the Leeds and Liverpool Canal in West Yorkshire. The total rise here is 60 feet (18 metres). A staircase such as this would have needed many different types of craftsmen and workers to complete it. The boat 'Sam', in the foreground, is a maintenance craft, possibly waiting to load some items from the canal carpenters' shop (about 1910).*

22. *Aqueducts posed many problems for the canal builder. Often they had long embankments, which had to be stabilised. The canal had to be watertight, for a leaking waterway could cause a landslip with terrible consequences. This is the 200 yard (182 metre) long Bulls Bridge Aqueduct in Derbyshire on the Cromford Canal over the river Amber, a railway and a road. Here high brick retaining walls had been built on top of an earth embankment. The light swing bridge in the foreground allows the towpath to change sides. The water tank on the railway receives its supply from the canal.*

23. *The Barton Swing Aqueduct carries the Bridgewater Canal over the Manchester Ship Canal. Designed by Sir Edward Leader, it replaces Brindley's original structure. When required to open, this entire structure, weighing some 1450 tons, is swung sideways. The towpath on the left is raised, and a horse is pulling the narrowboat in the foreground. The aqueduct is closed for two weeks every year for maintenance.*

24. *Tunnels were usually driven from several different points. The navvies would start at each end and also dig from a number of points along the route and tunnel out from there. The downshafts were used for taking out the spoil. Once the tunnels were opened many downshafts were bricked around and used for ventilation. Others were filled in but were often opened up again with the coming of powered craft with their smoky exhausts. This photograph shows tunnel repairs at Blisworth in 1914.*

25. The most famous canal lift is at Anderton in Cheshire, which drops boats from the Trent and Mersey Canal down 50 feet (15 metres) to the river Weaver. It was opened in 1875 and as originally designed (seen here) worked on the principle of counterbalanced caissons. Later it was converted to electric operation so that the caissons could move singly. There was much trade between the Weaver and the Trent and Mersey, and the lift did away with the need for expensive transhipment.

26. Two boats could fit into the caissons of the Anderton Lift. The descending caisson was designed to force up the other caisson by hydraulic action. An extra 6 inches (150 mm) of water was added to the downward caisson to make it heavier. This picture, taken in the 1940s, shows a pair of Fellows Morton and Clayton boats leaving the lift for the River Weaver.

heavy clay puddle. One of the most spectacular aqueducts, the Pontcysyllte over the river Dee near Ruabon in Clwyd, was completed in 1805 and was over 1000 feet (300 metres) long with nineteen arches of 45 feet (14 metres) span. Here an iron trough was built on masonry piers and at its highest it is 121 feet (37 metres) above the valley floor. An unusual form of aqueduct is one which crosses a river almost at water level. Here a chamber is built in the river under the point where the canal would cross it. A weir is built upstream of it, the effect being a siphon enabling the water to pass under the canal. The Whitewater Aqueduct on the Basingstoke Canal is a good example of this type.

Where a canal builder could not avoid crossing high ground, a tunnel was sometimes necessary. Harecastle Tunnel, on the Trent and Mersey Canal in Staffordshire, was only 9 feet (2.7 metres) wide and 12 feet (3.7 metres) high. The longest canal tunnel is at Standedge on the Huddersfield Narrow Canal. It is 3 miles (4.8 km) long and is 644 feet (196 metres) above sea level.

27. The most famous inclined plane to be built in Britain was at Foxton in Leicestershire. Opened in 1900, it bypassed ten locks with a rise of 75 feet (23 metres). Two caissons, 80 feet (24.3 metres) by 15 feet (4.6 metres) by 5 feet (1.5 metres) deep, capable of taking two narrowboats each, were hauled up and down the plane on rails. The two caissons almost couterbalanced each other, but there was always a steam engine to help counteract friction. One of the caissons is seen at the top of the slope, whilst in the foreground the other is submerged in the canal. Lifting the guillotine gate will give access for the boats. The lift closed in 1912 because of lack of traffic.

28. *This view of Greenberfield on the Leeds and Liverpool Canal typifies the country canal scene — the waterway winding round the hillside, the lock and the two overbridges. Overbridges were an important part of the canal landscape. Here they are made of local stone with stone abutments, but more often they were made of brick. The arch is picked out in white to help boats that are navigating by night. In 1820 the single two-lock riser originally built here was replaced by single locks on a short deviation. The old course, including a bridge and a lock cottage, can be seen in the centre of the picture.*

29. *Many bridges were cheaply made. They were either lifting bridges or swing bridges. They were made of wood and required no embankment either side. The problems with these were the high cost of maintenance and the fact that each boat would have to stop for the crew to operate the bridge and then stop again to pick up the crew. The narrowboat 'Blue Lias', owned by Kaye and Company of Southam and loaded with cement, is seen passing through a bridge which is crossed by the appropriately named Draw Bridge Road at Shirley, near Birmingham, on the Stratford-on-Avon Canal in 1923.*

30. *Lock-keepers' cottages were usually quite conventional small houses but on the Thames and Severn and the Staffordshire and Worcestershire canals some of them were built as roundhouses. This is Gailey on the Staffordshire and Worcestershire, photographed in 1951. It is not known why they were this shape, although the lock-keeper has a good view of approaching traffic from the upper windows. The tunnel under the road carries the towpath. Because of road widening on the A5 the beams of the lower lock gates have been truncated.*

Another way of overcoming steep natural obstacles was the canal lift or inclined plane. Most of these were designed before engineering skills and construction materials could match the ingenuity of the design. Even the Foxton Inclined Plane near Market Harborough, Leicestershire, which replaced a staircase of locks (two batches of five) and opened as late as 1900, suffered from the continual breaking of the rails on which the caissons ran because of the extreme weight they had to carry. Except on the industrial tub-boat canals, where the boats were taken up a slope on wheels, most canal lifts and planes take up a boat floating in water, hence the enormous weight.

The commonest feature found on the canals is the over-bridge. Roads existed before the canals and had to be taken over the water. The construction of a canal often divided farms, and so accommodation bridges had to be built to enable the farmer or landowner to reach his fields. These bridges are not so strongly made, and later, with the coming of the traction engine, cast iron notices warning of weight restrictions had to be erected. Most bridges were made of the local stone or bricks, though some, such as lifting bridges and swing bridges, were made of wood. On the Oxford Canal there are examples of beautiful cast iron over bridges.

It was necessary for the canal company to build other structures, including cottages to house lock-keepers. Most of these were of the usual shape but some were built as watch-towers, so that the keeper could see if any craft were approaching. Wharves and warehouses were often the responsibility of the canal company as well as the cranes and other equipment there.

31. *The Basingstoke Canal was one of the many waterways opened during the days of canal mania but never completed as a through route. Originally it had been intended to form part of an inland waterway route to Southampton, but there was never enough trade to keep it viable. This 1905 photograph of Basingstoke Wharf shows how a canal silts up and becomes covered in weed if maintenance is neglected.*

3. Operating and maintenance

The principal maintenance problem is keeping the water in its designed channel. In between the summit and the lowest level of the canal it acts as a drain for all the water coming off the surrounding land. In times of heavy rain it would be easy for the canal to overflow its banks and cause flooding. The lengthman would repeatedly patrol his stretch of canal, opening sluices to let off surplus water, unblocking overflow weirs and looking out for weak spots. A major burst could arise from something as small as a rat hole. The lengthman would know all the features of his piece of canal. In summer he would regulate incoming water to try to keep the levels up and he would look after the towpath, most important in the days of horse-drawn boats, and deal with hedging and ditching. The boundary fence was nearly always the responsibility of the canal company.

The lock-keeper's job was not so much to help a boat through the lock, but to keep the structure in good working order: keeping the paddle gear well greased and the paddles and the bypass stream clear of obstructions. If there was any damage to the lock equipment, the lock-keeper would have to try and mend it or call in help from the maintenance yard. Each stretch of canal would have its own maintenance workshop, where blacksmiths, carpenters, bricklayers and other artisans would be based. Usually the maintenance gang would be out mending something, often miles from home. At some maintenance workshops, lock gates would be made and paddle gear repaired. The maintenance men could turn their hand to almost anything.

The dredging gang was also based at the workshop. Canals were continually silting up and had to be dredged. At first the crude spoon dredger was used, then the steam grab and later diesel and hydraulic equipment. Dredging has to be done in a controlled manner, and the grab must not dredge too deeply or it will go through the clay puddle base and cause the canal to leak. Usually the dredgings had to be taken away by water and dumped elsewhere. Bank protection work is part of the maintenance programme, including piledriving and backfilling. Like dredging, this often takes place on stretches of the canal that are a long way from the nearest road, so all the materials and equipment are brought in by water.

In winter all hands worked to keep the canal open when it froze over. Crushed ice behind lock gates made them difficult to open.

32. This photograph was taken in 1948 on the Leigh branch of the Leeds and Liverpool Canal near Bickershaw Colliery. It shows the maintenance gang trying to locate a leak, which was found to be a very sizable hole. As a result of mining subsidence the canal at this point is about 20 feet (6 metres) deep. Colliery waste is being used to increase the height of the banks. Mining subsidence was always a great source of trouble to maintenance teams in colliery areas.

33. On river navigations flooding was a serious problem. While there may never have been much commercial traffic here on the upper reaches of the Thames at Lechlade, flooding caused great disruption to traffic on rivers like the Trent, the Severn and the Soar. Boatmen who knew the channel could take powered craft across the fields or up the course of the river. Horse-drawn craft were at a standstill as the towpaths were covered with water.

34 (opposite, top). *When lock repairs were more than the lock-keeper could do himself the maintenance gangs were called in. This is a major stoppage on the Hanwell flight in London. The sheerlegs over the lock show that the gates are being changed. The workboat in the foreground is full of cement and sand for the new brickwork. The craft behind has on it a steam-driven pump which is pumping out water that has seeped into the drained lock chamber. The presence of numerous bystanders suggests that this was a weekend stoppage.*

35 (opposite, bottom). *One night in October 1939 3 inches (76 mm) of rain fell in the Weedon area of Northamptonshire. The lengthman was up all night but was unable to let off enough of the surplus water and a breach occurred in a weak spot in an embankment on the Grand Union Canal. This was then probably Britain's busiest waterway for long-distance traffic, and repairs to the breach would normally take months. In a very short time, however, the maintenance gang built a temporary channel, supported by piling tied back to posts driven into the sound bank.*

36 (below). *Many canal banks are quite wide and grow a lot of vegetation. This could be a good source of hay, which could either be sold or used by the canal companies for the horses. This scene is on the Bridgwater and Taunton Canal in Somerset, near Huntworth. One of the craft peculiar to that waterway has been enlarged with the addition of outriggers to carry this extra light but bulky cargo.*

Canals and Waterways

37 (left). *An essential crafts-man was the lock-gate maker. This man is seen at work in the yard at Tardebigge on the Worcester and Birmingham Canal. For nearly two hundred years the lock gates were made of wood, but nowadays many are made from welded steel. Each lock was a little different from the next, either in width or more usually depth, so no two lock gates were likely to be the same. Many lock gates have the date of manufacture carved into them, and it is not uncommon to find bottom gates, in particu-lar, which are fifty or more years old.*

38 (below). *Among the many skills exercised in the mainte-nance yard is that of the tin-smith. These tinsmiths, seen at Ellesmere Port in 1892, would have undertaken all sorts of light metalwork and it appears that the repair of lamps was one of their main tasks. It is prob-able that there was a small forge in this workshop where bolts would be made. The man on the left is holding a thread-cutting tool.*

39. *Maintenance yards are spaced out along the canal system, and it is from these that repairs are organised. This is Hatton Yard on the Grand Union Canal in Warwickshire, photographed in 1934. An assortment of old lock gates and other items are on the wharfside and two maintenance boats are alongside carrying part of a steam piling rig. On the left is the steam tug 'De Salis', built by Bushell Brothers in 1923, which had just been taken out of service because tunnel towing was no longer necessary as most craft were motorised. In the 1930s the Grand Union Canal Company modernised the route to Birmingham, including widening the locks. A pair of boats is seen leaving the modernised locks on the Hatton flight of 21 locks. The old locks on the right are being used as a dry dock.*

Whilst a metal boat could pierce several inches of ice, a wooden boat would be torn to pieces by it. For icebreaking a specially constructed horse-drawn boat was rocked through the ice, clearing quite a wide path. Later, power-driven icebreakers or tugs were used.

Keeping the canal open was vital. Essential repairs were, however, necessary and so these 'stoppages' were carefully planned, often over a bank holiday weekend. Sometimes boats could take another route avoiding the stoppage, but often they could not, and queues of boats would moor up waiting for the job to end. The maintenance gang would work shifts around the clock to get the work done. There would be occasions when the stoppage had to be a long one, such as for repairs in the middle of a tunnel, where there would be special problems. In this case notification of a long closure was sent out well in advance. On

40 (above). *In winter the canal had to be kept open despite the freezing conditions. At first the icebreaking was done by a specially constructed boat towed by a team of horses. In this scene a steam-driven icebreaker is being used on the Leeds and Liverpool Canal at Gargrave, North Yorkshire, helped by a horse-drawn craft. Icebreakers were usually built with rounded bilges instead of a flat bottom, thus allowing the boat to be rocked from side to side, so breaking a wide channel through the ice.*

41 (opposite, top). *When overbridges required rebuilding, it was usually done in the same manner in which the bridge had been built originally. A wooden former in the shape of the arch was first made and the bridge was rebuilt over this. This would have been done in such a way as to allow boats still to pass underneath. This is bridge 77 at Linford Wharf, Buckinghamshire. The Newport Pagnell branch (1¼ miles, 2 km long) used to leave under the bridge on the right. This branch, built in 1817, was closed in 1863.*

42 (opposite, bottom). *The coming of the steam dredger greatly speeded the process of keeping the channel deep and clear, but dredging was only as quick as the horse-drawn mudboats could take away and unload the dredgings. Here at Braunston, Northampton-shire, in 1908 the dredger is seen on the left, unusually close to the steam grab on the bank which unloads the dredgings. The dredger cannot just dump its dredgings anywhere. The firebox and boiler of the floating dredger were situated in the cabin area behind the crane and it must have been very hot work stoking the boiler.*

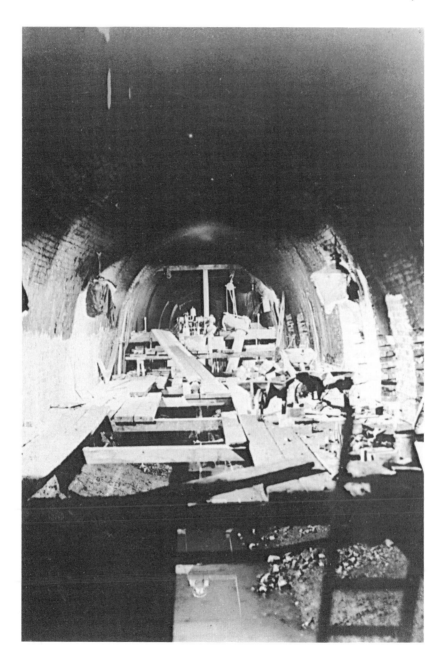

43 (opposite). *Repairs to tunnels can often cause long delays to boat traffic. Underwater repairs require the draining of the tunnel and the setting up of coffer dams. This is Blisworth tunnel, Northamptonshire, in 1914. The shape of the invert (floor) is clearly shown. The problems of getting equipment into these confined spaces must have been considerable.*

44 (below). *The mainstay of the maintenance of any canal is the gang of men working away from the yard doing general repairs. This scene is on the Peak Forest Canal at Furness Vale, Derbyshire. It looks as if they have been undertaking piling of the canal bank and filling in behind. Maintenance craft such as this were often former working boats though sometimes they were made especially for the job. The cabin was a useful shelter during inclement weather and a place for brewing up.*

45 (above). *This photograph of the Grand Junction Canal at Hanwell, London, dated around 1910 is taken from a picture postcard entitled 'The Annual Clean-Out'. It implies that the annual stoppage on the canal was well known to the locals, who came down to play and probe in the mud. It can be clearly seen that the deep channel of a canal runs straight down the middle and that it is very shallow towards the bank. Two laden boats passing here would scrape along the bed of the canal.*

46 (opposite, top). *Thomas Telford built the London to Holyhead road. Later, when he was building the Shropshire Union Canal he had to cross this road near Stretton north of Wolverhampton. This short aqueduct was made in the form of a cast iron trough, seen here under repair in the 1950s. As on the Pontcysyllte Aqueduct, the towpath sticks out over the trough, allowing a flow of water alongside the boat. A narrow trough would slow the boat down. This repair is obviously part of a big stoppage, as the canal is drained.*

47 (opposite, bottom). *Even though a bank holiday stoppage was scheduled, it still caused hold-ups where there was no alternative route for the boats to take. Here a traffic jam is building up at the bottom of the Stoke Bruerne flight of locks at the Easter stoppage in 1907. The boat in the foreground is fully loaded with timber, as is the one against the bank. Both show a little freeboard compared with the deeply laden coal boat beside the far timber boat. The two boats against the right-hand bank appear to be unladen.*

occasions when there was a breach in the canal bank, for instance, there would have to be an instant stoppage, with no warning. This would badly upset the working of the waterways, often leaving boats stranded for weeks at a time.

Many different types of craft were used by the maintenance department, including dredgers, icebreakers and mudboats, and all of these had to be looked after, so the maintenance yard was equipped with boat-repairing facilities, the most important of which was the dry dock.

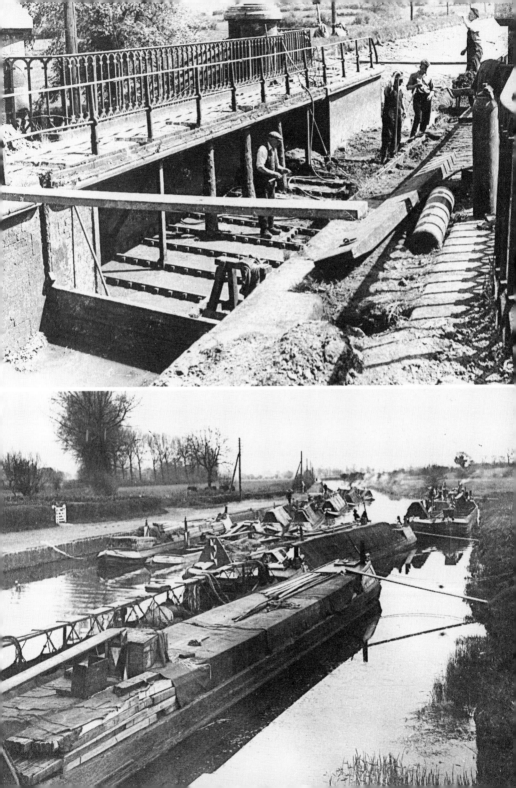

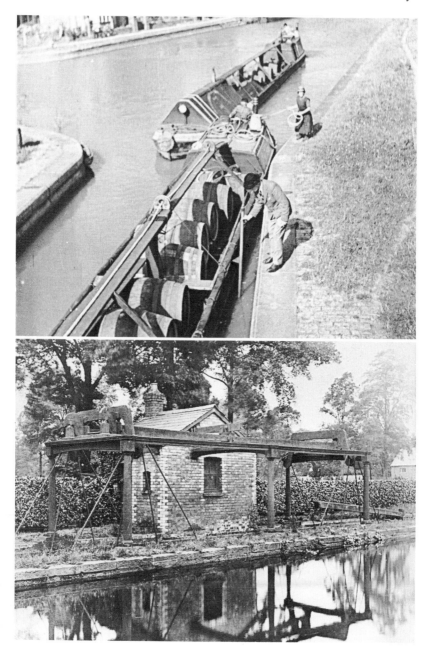

48 (opposite, top). *The principal income of a canal company came from tolls charged to the carriers. Each type of cargo had a going rate but the canal company could not rely on the information provided by the boat crew as to the weight of the cargo. To overcome possible dishonesty boat 'gauging' took place. Here the toll clerk measures the freeboard of a laden boat. The instrument used consists of a float moving in a graduated tube which is fitted with a right-angle bracket. The toll clerk had a list of the boats' 'first gauging', which was taken when the boats were built. From this he would work out the weight of cargo being carried.*

49 (opposite, bottom). *Another way of ascertaining the weight of the cargo of a boat was the boat-weighing machine. Few of these were built because of the cost and the time taken to weigh the boat. They were usually reserved for boats which the canal company suspected of evading tolls. This weighing machine was first built on the Glamorganshire canal at Tongwynlais in 1836 and later it was rebuilt at North Road, Cardiff. It came out of use after one hundred years. This picture was taken in 1950. The boat floated over the cradle of the machine, the water was drained out, and the full weight of the boat was then carried on the weighing cradle.*

50 (above). *One of the services which the canal company had to provide was a means of getting an unpowered horseboat through a tunnel. Legging was slow, so steam tugs were employed at a number of tunnels. The tunnel tugs ran to a timetable and towed a train of horseboats behind. Here, at Blisworth, Northamptonshire, about 1910, the tunnel tug is almost obscured by its own smoke in the middle of the photograph. The horseboats on the right are waiting for towage, whilst a steam-powered narrowboat and butty pass by, having no need for the tug's services.*

51 (following page). *A rare photograph of legging shows canal workmen propelling a boat through Butterley Tunnel on the Cromford Canal in Derbyshire. The date is thought to be around 1900, a time when the tunnel was closed by its owners, the Midland Railway Company, as a result of mining subsidence. They had to wait a number of years before it could be officially abandoned and in the intervening time it had to be maintained. When it was in commercial use, this 3000 yard (2743 metre) tunnel was a bottleneck as a boat would take as much as three hours to be legged through it.*

52 (above). *The North Wilts Canal was opened from Swindon to Cricklade in 1819, joining the Thames and Severn Canal with the Wilts and Berks Canal. One of the principal traffics was coal from the Somerset coalfields. The canal was in trouble from 1874 but struggled on until 1906, when the last boat passed. Maintenance had been at a very low level for years, so it is not surprising to find the abandoned canal very quickly silted up. This is Rodbourne Road Bridge in Swindon, about 1914.*

53 (opposite, top). *The Swansea Canal was sold to the Great Western Railway in 1873 for £107,000. At this time it was still showing a good profit. Trade ceased on the upper sections around 1900 but short-haul traffic on the lower reaches continued until 1931. No profits had, however, been made since 1912, so maintenance was kept to a minimum. This photograph was taken on 2nd October 1934 and shows the course of the canal east of the Great Western Railway's Swansea High Street station. This is close to the termination of the canal and the view looks down to the North Dock at a time when the canal was being filled in.*

54 (opposite, bottom). *The Barnsley Canal, whose main traffic was always coal, was opened in 1799. Its closure in 1953 was due to coal-mining subsidence. One of the features of the canal was the massive Barnsley Aqueduct, shown here after it had been demolished as unsafe in 1953. A number of canals have closed because of the failure of a structure such as a tunnel or bridge before the waterway had finished its useful life as a trade route.*

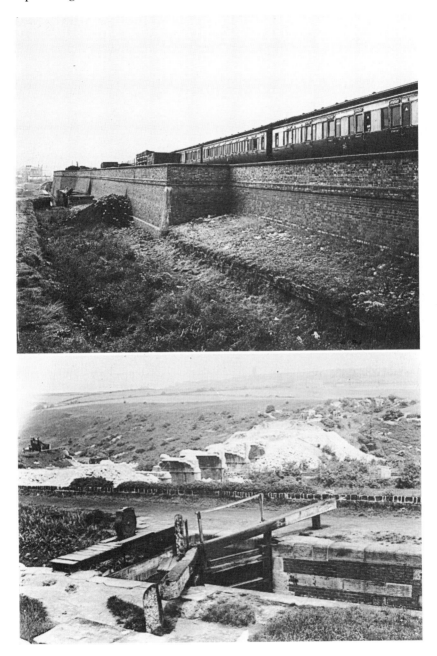

Besides maintenance the company had to provide other services for boatmen. Most importantly they needed to collect the revenue to keep the company going. The principal source of income was from the boats themselves. Until after the Second World War tolls were charged much as they had been on the road system. Tolls were either collected by special toll clerks or on less busy routes by lock-keepers. Canals also supplied vast quantities of water for industrial use and this provided a good income. A service peculiar to canals was that of the leggers at certain tunnels. Tunnels lacked towpaths (and even if they had them, the horses would not pass through them) and an alternative motive power was necessary. Tunnel leggers lay on boards stretching out from the boat towards the tunnel's sides and literally walked the boat through with their feet pushing against the walls. On some canals the boatmen had to do this themselves. With the coming of steam propulsion tunnel tugs were employed instead.

Canal companies which had their own trading fleets, such as the Grand Union, required extra staff to do the office work and obtain the cargoes. There would be engineers and other craftsmen to service the motors and repair the boats, and the company would also have to employ boatmen to crew the vessels.

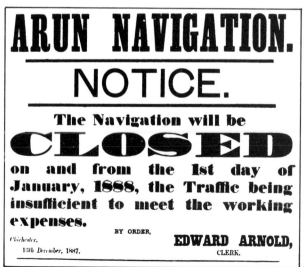

ARUN NAVIGATION.

NOTICE.

The Navigation will be

CLOSED

on and from the 1st day of January, 1888, the Traffic being insufficient to meet the working expenses.

BY ORDER,

Chichester,
13th December, 1887.

EDWARD ARNOLD,
CLERK.

55. *Because there was not enough money coming in from boats trading on the waterway to pay the expenses, the Arun Navigation closed in 1887, one hundred years after it had opened. There was still some traffic on the lower reaches until 1938, but others paid the cost of upkeep — the navigation company had long gone.*

4. The boats

When Brindley determined the size of a lock, he also dictated the lengths and width of the canal boats. At the same time he must have decided how deep the canal was going to be, so a prospective boatbuilder knowing the depth, length and breadth, had the outline for a narrowboat. During the building of a canal water-borne craft of some form were required to move equipment along the incomplete waterway. These boats were probably made as and when required by the carpenters on contract or by local labour. The 'starvationers', the craft on the Duke of Bridgewater's Canal, were simple to build, and the first narrowboats were probably of similar construction. Engravings of the 1820s by reputable artists show that the narrowboat had developed much as we know it today. No doubt the first boatbuilders were carpenters and craftsmen who had businesses in the villages through which the waterway passed. They would have adapted very quickly to the requirements of the carriers.

The requirements for a narrowboat were that it should 'swim' well in the water, steer well and carry as much cargo as possible, which was about 25 tons. The craft were completely utilitarian, but even so many had graceful lines. Wood was the universal material used for their construction. The side planks were of oak, as they were subject to getting wet and dry alternately, depending on whether the boat was laden or not. The bottom of the boat was made of elm, a wood which when continually submerged is immensely strong: most boat bottoms wore out through contact with the bed of the canal rather than as a result of structural failure. When a hull was constructed 'chalicoe', a mixture of tar, cow hair and horse dung, was plastered all over it and encased in light vertical planks. Gaps in the outer planking were sealed with oakum, which was forced into them and up against the vertical planks. Finally the outside of the craft was covered in tar. Over the years techniques changed, particularly with the coming of the motor boat. Craft began to be made of steel or sometimes with composite metal sides with elm bottoms, and so the skills of the boatyards changed.

When a hull had been made it had to be equipped with 'cloths' or sheets, the tarpaulins which kept the cargo from getting wet. If the boatyard did not have the facility to make these, they had to buy them in, as with ropes and fenders. Each boat had a bow fender, to protect the craft in the lock and also to protect the lock

56 (above). *The first boats were built on the canal bank by local craftsmen and carpenters. Their premises would have been extremely crude and very similar to this scene on the banks of the Basingstoke Canal at Ash Vale, Surrey, amazingly as recently as 1932.*

57 (left). *The first narrowboats were the 'strarvationers' or mine boats from the Duke of Bridgewater's Canal. They are of very simple construction, with exposed wooden knees. This photograph, taken long after the Worsley mines were closed, shows two National Coal Board workmen on maintenance duties in the Worsley Mine basin. The sluice that they are operating was originally used to create a current within the mines to flush the boats out.*

58. *Narrowboats soon found their own style. The boats on the canals of South Wales, cut off from the Midlands, retained the style of the 'starvationers'. These boats were 60 feet (18 metres) long and of 9 feet (2.7 metres) beam, carrying 24 tons on a draft of 2 feet 9 inches (0.84 metres). This scene in 1912 is at Swansea Bridge on the Neath Canal. The boats were deliberately built double-ended so that there was no need to turn them round. Like the narrowboats, they had oak sides and elm bottoms. On canal boats in the Midlands, iron later replaced wood for the knees.*

59. *Thomas Shepherd produced a number of engravings of the canal scene in 1827. They were remarkably detailed. Many crews did not start living on their boats until the railway competition was being strongly felt and this may explain the small cabin. The large rudder was typical of the Thames barge and has gradually been reduced in size over the years. The diamond design is thought to be the trademark of Pickfords, a company which left canal carrying in the 1840s for land-based haulage.*

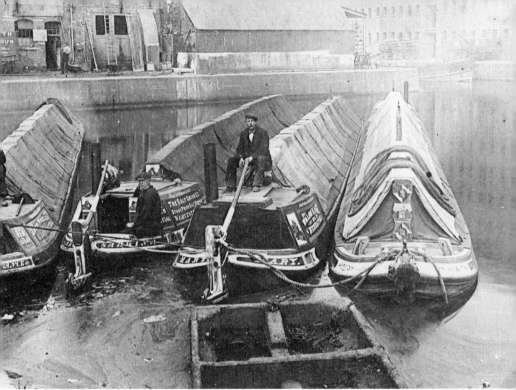

60. *The narrowboat was the versatile craft of the narrow canals of Britain. These four boats are in Gloucester Docks waiting to unload their cargo, probably of salt. The foretimbers on the boat on the right show that it was used to travelling on the river Severn. The boats are well decorated, the decorations on the cratch (or end of the cargo hold) of the boat on the right being unusual. 'Mary' has a decorative horsetail on the rudder. 'Sabrina' has a decorative barrel on the cabin top for drinking water, something more familiar to boats on northern waterways. All boats have their tillers in the upright position, denoting that they are moored up. This also gives added clearance under the tiller for getting in or out of the cabin.*

61. *Close to Hawkesbury Junction on the Oxford Canal in Warwickshire stood the former boatyard of Sephton of Tusses Bridge. This is a typical canalside boatbuilder's yard. A rough shed covers only part of one boat, while another boat lies on the slip in the open. This boat comes from the fleet of J. and E. Morton of Milnsbridge, a firm which carried cargoes of chemicals in carboys — hence the unusual partitioning of the hull.*

62. *Nearly all canal boats were brightly painted and most crews took pride to see that the paint remained in good order for as long as possible. This Samuel Barlow boat shows the traditional roses around the lettering and castles on the end of the cabin side. There are geometric designs on the counter and the rudder. There would have been more roses and castles on the cabin doors.*

63. *A variety of narrowboats moored up at the top of the Anderton Lift on a Sunday morning in the 1930s. The lift did not operate on a Sunday. Most of the boats are returning empty from the Potteries, making for Weston Point Docks on the river Weaver to load raw materials. The cargo space is clearly seen with the cratch at the bow and the stands down the centre of the hold to support the top planks, properly set out on the boat in the centre alongside the left-hand bank. The crossplanks are called stretchers and stop the sides of the boat from expanding sideways.*

64 (above). *Sail was an unusual motive power on the narrow canals. A few narrowboats operating off the Trent on the Chesterfield Canal carried sail, but they were the exception. On the wide Yorkshire waterways it was more common. Many Humber keels were rigged to take a mainsail and a topsail, though the latter is not shown here. These craft could carry between 60 and 80 tons. They were basically flat-bottomed with only a very small keel. They tended to use leeboards when working to windward.*

65 (opposite, top). *If a keel had been proceeding under sail and the wind dropped there was no alternative but to shaft the craft along. A Yorkshire keel is seen here being shafted at Hexthorpe Flats, Doncaster. Manpower is the oldest power source in the world. On a narrow waterway, if the horse failed the only alternative was bow-hauling by the crew themselves. In the foreground there is a boat station where Edwardians and their ladies could go for a row on the water.*

66 (opposite, bottom). *The horse was the basic motive power on the canals for the first 150 or so years. A variety of horses was used. The Shire was probably the most popular, but also used were Clydesdales, the Suffolk Punch and latterly the Percheron. This scene in 1907 shows two horse-drawn boats approaching the top lock at Stoke Bruerne on the Grand Junction Canal in Northamptonshire. A loaded boat is coming out of the lock. Four other fully loaded boats are moored on the right. The towpath is wide and well kept and the horse droppings are very evident, as they were all over the canal system.*

gate from damage by the boat, and a 'tipcat' fender on the stern, to protect the projecting rudder from damage. A number of different ropes would be required, including a light towing line for the horse, a heavy towing line for when the boat was being tugged through a tunnel and heavier mooring lines.

The painting of the boat was also most important. Each yard had its own style, but the traditional subject matter was nearly always the same: 'roses and castles', lakes and symbols from a pack of cards. Each boat carried its name and the name of the owner, whether a company or a 'number one' (an owner operator). Everything was as bright and colourful as possible to counter the drabness of the Victorian urban landscape in which the boats operated for much of the time.

For the first 150 years or so motive power was provided by a horse, mule or donkey. If the boatman owned the horse or always worked with the same one there was usually a special relationship between them, but where a company provided change horses at intervals there was no such rapport and the horses suffered.

67 (opposite). *Mules and donkeys were also used to haul boats but were never as popular as horses. Donkeys often worked in pairs and were mainly confined to the waterways of the West Midlands. Donkeys were noted for being very sure-footed. In this 1930s photograph, a mule is seen pulling a loaded narrowboat on the Trent and Mersey Canal near Northwich, Cheshire. Mules were first used on the waterways of northern England. The first boat to move on the Bridgewater Canal was apparently drawn by a mule.*

68 (below). *The coming of steam to the canal system in 1864 did not cause the revolution that was expected. The loss of cargo space did not suit the majority of carriers. It did, however, allow a butty to be towed. In this photograph an unknown steamer of the Fellows, Morton and Clayton fleet is seen with the butty 'Boxmoor' at Rickmansworth Lock. Coming out of the lock is a horse-drawn boat. The horse is decked out in traditional style with coloured bobbins down its side to stop chafing and is contentedly feeding from a bowl whilst working. The ribbed towpath is to give the horse more grip when passing under the bridge. The passing of thousands of horse-drawn boats has rubbed great grooves in the metal protector fitted to the brick of the bridge on the left.*

69. *A typical scene on the Midland canals. A pair of working boats photographed in August 1935 in the Hatton Flight in Warwickshire. The boats are 'Bramble' and 'Bascote' of the Fellows, Morton and Clayton fleet, crewed by Albert and Emma Russon. On the left the motorboat is just over a year old, having been built at the yard of W. J. Yarwood and Sons of Northwich and fitted out at the Fellows, Morton and Clayton yard at Uxbridge. The motor is housed in its own small cabin forward of the living quarters. Motorboats had smaller rudders and metal tube tillers, as opposed to the butty's large wooden rudder and tiller. The latter is disconnected in this picture.*

70. *On the Regent's Canal in London there was a lot of traffic up from Regent's Canal Dock, including both long-haul traffic in narrowboats and local traffic in dumb barges and lighters. Much of the local traffic was horse-drawn. In the early 1950s the Docks and Inland Waterways Board experimented with tractor haulage but this proved unpopular. One or two of the tractors were even painted with roses and castles. They were equipped with a quick release for the tow-rope, for if a boat overran the tractor it could have pulled it into the water.*

71. On the lower Grand Junction Canal a number of wide narrowboats were used. They were 10 or 11 feet (3.05 to 3.35 metres) wide. They operated as far north as Braunston. Their disadvantages were that they could not pass an oncoming boat in a tunnel, they also took up a lock on their own and, where a canal had a narrow channel, tended either to run aground or put aground any boat they were passing. This boat, 'Langley', was built at Bushell Brothers yard at Tring on the Wendover branch for T. W. Toovey of Kings Langley.

72. During the 1930s the Grand Union Canal Company widened the locks between Braunston and Birmingham to give a wide-beam canal all the way from London. They did not, however, alter the width of the tunnels. With the problems already encountered over many years with wide boats, it seems surprising that the Grand Union Canal Company decided in 1934 to build a prototype of a new type of wide motorboat. They planned a fleet of these 66 ton capacity craft. 'Progress' was built at Bushell Brothers' yard at Tring. It went against all previous experience by using a Junkers diesel engine and wheel steering. This photograph was taken immediately after launching.

By the mid nineteenth century engineers were experimenting with steam propulsion, but only one company, Fellows, Morton and Clayton, ever ran a large fleet of steam craft. The steam engine and boiler weighed 10 tons, so reducing cargo-carrying capacity, and also required a larger than normal crew. These boats tended to work fly (non-stop) on the broad trunk canals between London and the Midlands carrying the more perishable cargoes. Otherwise steam was little used except for powering the tugs used in tunnels and for towing a number of boats on lock-free stretches of canal.

Motorboats started to appear after the First World War. They were not much faster than horse-drawn boats, but the additional power allowed an unpowered craft to be towed behind. Horses had been able to haul two boats only on well maintained and wide canals. The towed craft was usually called a 'butty' and was often a formerly horse-drawn wooden boat. A number of wooden boats

73. This 1910 photograph shows a very busy scene at Runcorn in Cheshire, the original terminus of the Bridgewater Canal. On the right are the Bridgewater Canal steam tugs. Built of wrought iron, they were introduced in 1875. They towed trains of flats and keels on the lockless stretches of the Bridgewater Canal and on the river Mersey and the Manchester Ship Canal. In the centre is a horse-drawn Mersey flat, the principal barge-size craft of the North-west. Narrowboats can also be seen.

were also converted to motorcraft. The first engines were single-cylinder Bolinder semi-diesels, which had a most distinctive exhaust note. Later multi-cylinder diesels became popular. A problem caused by the coming of the powered craft was that their wash badly eroded the canal banks and so much more maintenance was needed, especially steel piling and dredging.

At first the canal companies were not allowed to operate commercial carrying craft on the canal. The operators, one of the largest of which was Pickfords, paid the canal company tolls for the use of the waterway. Later the legislation was changed to permit the canal companies to operate their own fleets, some of which became very large. When canals were taken over by railway companies, these companies often had fleets of boats. Many firms which used the waterways had fleets of their own, rather than rely on contractors. Cowburn and Cowper, for example, transported their own chemicals and the cement manufacturer Charles Nelson of Warwickshire also had its own craft. By far the greatest users of the canals were the independent carriers. Most of them carried general cargoes but others specialised, such as Samuel Barlow in coal, or J. and G. Meakin in pottery materials. Owner operators, of which there were many, were known as 'number ones'. They tended to trade over regular routes carrying the same types of cargo, as it was difficult for them to arrange new trade.

Most cargo could be carried in narrowboats of a standard design but one company, Thomas Clayton from Oldbury, West Midlands, specialised in the carrying of liquids. These often consisted of various grades of oil or the products of gasworks. The boats for this trade were built as floating tanks, which gave them a distinctive low line when loaded.

74 (following page, top). *To compete with the railways in the mid 1860s, the Chief Engineer of the Aire and Calder Navigation, W. H. Bartholomew, had the idea of using trains of compartment boats (also known as 'Tom Puddings'), each carrying 35 to 40 tons of coal. Towed by a steam tug, these trains had some flexibility, as can be seen in this photograph, taken in 1950 near Pollington Lock, Goole. At Goole high hoists capable of lifting a loaded compartment boat were constructed to tip the loaded boat straight into the holds of coastal vessels.*

75 (following page, bottom). *At first some canals carried passengers but with the coming of the railways the running of packet boats gradually ceased. Some canals pass through very pretty scenery, and throughout Victorian and Edwardian times a few enterprising people ran trip boats on the waterways. The Ellesmere Canal (known as the Llangollen by most people) takes much of its water from the river Dee at Llangollen. The top 2 miles (3 km) of the canal, however, were never navigated by narrowboats, but from 1886 a horse-drawn trip boat has plied those waters. This view from the late 1920s is one of dozens of postcards which have been published of this craft.*

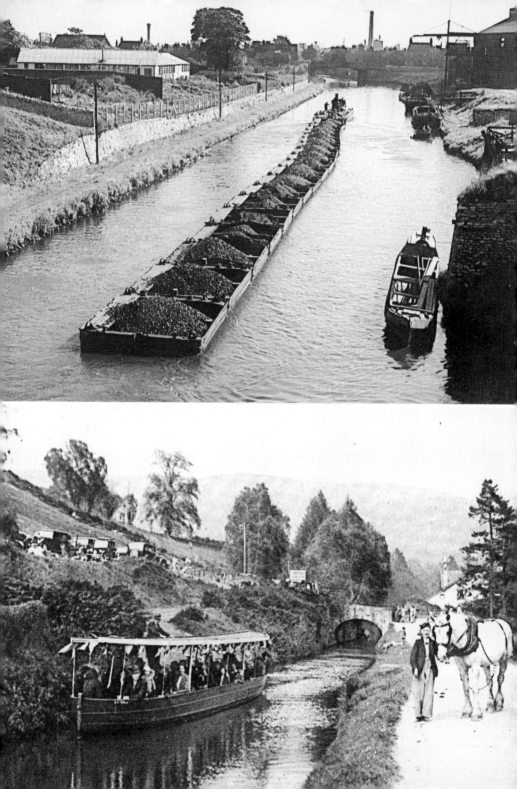

5. The cargoes

Coal was the staple fuel of the industrial revolution. Everyone wanted it, whether it was for domestic or commercial use. Before the canal age, coal was carried round the coast and up rivers. When canals were being built, they were often constructed to pass close to the collieries, so enabling the coal to be taken direct from the pit to the factory. This door-to-door service survived until 1972, the last regular long-haul traffic on the canals. Sometimes the collieries owned their own boats and did their own carrying.

Limestone was another very important traffic. The Peak Forest Canal and the Caldon Canal almost entirely depended on it. Limestone is the flux in the process of converting iron ore into molten metal. Later lime became one of the requirements of the burgeoning chemical industry. In many cases limekilns were set up alongside canals to process limestone which had come either by tramroad or by canal. The boats which brought in the raw material and the coal took away the processed lime. Like salt, another major requirement of the chemical industry, lime had to be kept dry. Usually the boats were loaded under cover at the wharf and they had to be well sheeted down and protected from the weather, as well as watertight from below.

Josiah Wedgwood was one of the first industrialists to see the great advantage of canal transport. The clay for his pottery works came up the Trent and Mersey Canal and coal was available locally. Other bulky substances are needed for pottery making, such as felspar, flint and bone. The finished products, when packed for travelling, were rather light so even a fully loaded boat carried only about 10 tons. Often these cargoes were left for specialist carriers.

Not all cargo was industrial: much of it was ordinary domestic goods. For many years some companies ran craft called fly boats which carried valuable and perishable cargo. These boats had no special facilities but usually travelled non-stop from start to destination. At one time all the other boats had to give way to them to help them speed on their journey. In certain areas companies ran passenger boats, mainly into large cities, but as the railways improved this traffic disappeared except for special occasions. Dozens of photographs exist of Sunday school and church outings being taken in canal boats, especially cleared for the purpose at the weekend.

76 (opposite, top). *A typical coal-carrying scene of a Samuel Barlow and Company boat from Birmingham. This company specialised in coal traffic on the Warwickshire waterways. The boat is loaded deep with slack boards at the stern of the cargo hold to allow the coal to be piled higher to make up for the lightness of the cabin. The top planks allow quick access to the fore end. The bicycle allows one of the crew to ride ahead to set locks for the boat. Most boats had dogs.*

77 (opposite, bottom). *More boats moved on the canals around Birmingham than anywhere else. Much of the traffic was coal from local pits. This photograph of 1910 shows Hednesford Basin on the Cannock Extension of the Wyrley and Essington Canal, where coal from at least two collieries was loaded. The coal came from the mines in small tubs. The standard-gauge trucks in the foreground carry narrow-gauge coal tubs from the nearby Cannock and Rugeley Colliery.*

78 (below). *Stewarts and Lloyds steel tubeworks at Coombeswood, in the heart of the Black Country. To reach it boats had to pass through the narrow bore of the 557 yard (509 metre) Gosty Hill Tunnel. In its heyday the works handled hundreds of thousands of tons of raw materials and finished products, eighty per cent of them going by water. In this photograph by Tom Rolt, taken in July 1949, can be seen several Birmingham day boats loaded with coal and a pair of long-distance boats manoeuvring in the foreground, probably going to load steel tubes.*

79. *The Caldon Canal in Staffordshire used to lead from Etruria to Uttoxeter, but the Froghall to Uttoxeter section was closed as early as 1846. The top lock of this section was, however, retained and when this photograph was taken, in 1910, two boats from the chemical firm Brunner-Mond were loading limestone. Froghall was one of the most significant limestone wharves. The stone came down by tramway from quarries over 3 miles (5 km) away. Limekilns are very evident, and the carriage of processed lime was also most important.*

80. *Stanton Ironworks, Derbyshire, on the banks of the Nutbrook and Erewash Canals, was a great consumer of coal and limestone. There was always a fleet of boats moored at the works. From this factory the finished product, often the famous Stanton pipes, was also taken away by water. The high cratch making a small compartment on the foredeck of the boat moored on the left was probably protecting the horse's fodder.*

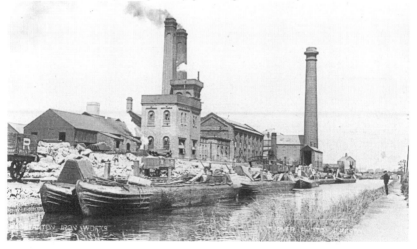

81. *The Anderton Canal Carrying Company was founded under that name in 1836 to trade in pottery materials, principally between the Stoke-on-Trent area and Runcorn or Weston Point Docks. The boat names were always carved into the top bend. Trade was good: at one time they had 175 narrowboats operating. The boat here is seen waiting for a cargo at Runcorn.*

82. *It became traditional that trading boats could quickly be converted when required for Sunday school, church or similar outings. This is the Lancaster Canal, about 1904. A canal boat had been requisitioned to carry a party from Friends School and was photographed returning from Levens. There is obviously another boat coming behind. The two horses are decked out in their full finery for this important occasion.*

83. *At one time there were over 1500 miles (2400 km) of horse-drawn tramways in England and Wales, many of which were built to serve the canals or inland waterways. The Little Eaton gangway from Denby and Kilburn Colliery down to the Little Eaton wharf on the Derby Canal was typical. This rare photograph of September 1908 at Denby Colliery was taken one year before the gangway closed. Unlike a railway, the flange was on the L-shaped rail and the wheels on the wagons had no flange.*

84. *The carriage of bulk liquids was left to specialists, of which Thomas Clayton of Oldbury was the largest, having a fleet of over sixty horse-drawn boats in the 1920s. These craft were in effect floating tanks, with the holds divided by baffles to avoid too much surge in the liquids. Nearly all the boats were made of wood. Here one of the fleet leaves a lock on the Napton Flight on the Oxford Canal.*

85. *Farmers did not often make use of the canals which passed through their land, but here sacks of threshed corn are being loaded on to narrowboats at Maids Moreton on the Buckingham branch of the Grand Junction Canal in 1900. They will most probably be taken direct to a mill. Ten years later parts of this branch were abandoned through lack of trade.*

86. *Coal was required by the private consumer as well as industry. Every canalside town had a number of coal merchants on the banks of the waterway; villages would often have one as well. This is the village wharf at Aynho on the Oxford Canal in 1905. The coal boat is being unloaded by hand and the coal taken to the storage area by wheelbarrow. A few canalside coal merchants still exist though they no longer get their supplies by boat. In the foreground is an overflow weir allowing surplus canal water to drain away into local streams.*

87. *Cadburys was a firm that used the waterways for the transport of raw and processed materials. This picture postcard issued by Cadburys depicts two horse-drawn boats on the Shropshire Union Canal in the 1920s, having collected milk from canalside farmers for use by the Cadbury factory at Knighton, Staffordshire. They also carried processed materials between Knighton and Bournville, Birmingham, and between Frampton on Severn, Gloucestershire, and Bournville. There was also long-distance traffic from Birmingham to London and Liverpool. At the height of trading the Cadburys fleet numbered seventeen, and their colours were chocolate and maroon.*

In many cases the canal could not reach the sources of the cargo — the mine or the quarry. To bring the raw material to the canal basin, tramroads were built. Most used horse-haulage though some had light locomotives. One of the earliest tramroads, built in 1777, ran from the quarries at Cauldon Lowe down to the Caldon Canal in Staffordshire, at Froghall Basin. Benjamin Outram was responsible for the Peak Forest Tramway (1796), which went from the Bugsworth Basin on the Peak Forest Canal to the limestone quarries at Dove Holes in Derbyshire.

Cargo handling, both loading and unloading, always tended to be primitive. The commonest handling equipment was a shovel and wheelbarrow. It might take two men half a day working flat out to empty a narrowboat of 25 tons of cargo. Simple cranes

88 (right). *Ellesmere Port grew from the small hamlet of Netherpool on the Wirral. The Shropshire Union Canal (previously the Birmingham and Liverpool Junction Canal) terminated here in 1835 with direct access to the river Mersey, and later to the Manchester Ship Canal. Hydraulic cranes were installed here in 1876, the pump powered by a Sir W. G. Armstrong and Company steam engine.*

89 (below). *After the Grand Union Canal had been modernised in the 1930s the canal company greatly expanded its own carrying fleet and encouraged others to do so. One of their principal destinations was Birmingham Quay, better known as Sampson Road Wharf. In 1937 a new warehouse is being built in the background. Mobile cranes and lorries speed the unloading and removal.*

90 (left). *In later years some mechanical aids were applied to coal traffic. This is Trafford Power Station, Manchester, where the coal is being drawn out of the hold by suction. This photograph was taken towards the end of the traffic in the mid 1960s. Power station coal was often dust, slack or very small lumps and so was ideal for this treatment. The same technique was often applied to cargoes of grain, another common canal cargo. The decoration on the Leeds and Liverpool short boat 'Irene' is typical.*

91 (opposite, top). *Canals did sometimes benefit from the railways. One such operation was the Great Western Railway sleeper depot at Hayes, Middlesex. Nearly all the timber used was delivered first to a London dock and then transported by barge to Hayes. The creosote to protect the sleepers was delivered direct to the yard by tank boats from the fleet of Claytons of Oldbury. The treated sleepers were usually taken away by railway.*

92 (opposite, bottom). *Regent's Canal Dock, London, was one of the principal places in Britain for the transhipment of cargoes which were brought in by ship either from around the British coast or, mainly, from overseas, into either lighters or barges for use locally in London. The cargoes for further inland went straight into narrowboats, several of which can be seen in this 1930 photograph.*

were sometimes available but grabs seldom were, so coal which might have been quickly loaded by gravity had to be laboriously unloaded by hand.

Canals did, for a time, benefit from their competitors. With the coming of the railways there was sometimes the opportunity to carry building materials and take away spoil. Roadstone was a profitable cargo for years. First there were occasional loads to country wharves for local road repairs; later in the nineteenth century, as road building improved and expanded, much road-stone traffic came down from quarries to locations near the new projects.

Imported cargoes shipped into docks such as London, Hull, Liverpool and Bristol were often unloaded straight into narrow-boats for onward transport inland. Sometimes the goods were stored on the wharfside and loaded when the narrowboat capacity was available. One of the last of these imports was barrels of lime juice unloaded at Brentford and taken up the Grand Union Canal to Boxmoor in Hertfordshire for the Roses factory. Narrowboats also carried cargoes down to the docks for export.

Where industry required a regular supply of raw materials, the canals were able to undercut the railways almost to the end. At Wolvercote Paper Mill near Oxford the wharf clerk kept good records, which still survive. In 1884 the mill was using around 100 tons of coal per week, all of which was brought in by water, coming from the Ashby Canal via the Coventry and Oxford Canals. The cost per ton for canal-borne coal in that year was 13s 4d. The wharf clerk had also worked out the cost if it had come by rail, including carriage by road from the sidings in Oxford, and this was 4d per ton more. In 1916 the rail cost remained more expensive, by 3¼d per ton. Wolvercote continued bringing in coal by water until May 1952, when the mill changed over to oil firing. The change to oil firing ended a number of coal-carrying contracts, while those that were left gradually switched to road for their supplies.

93. *Sometimes boats arrived at their destination in larger numbers than the wharf could cope with. One reason for this might be the arrival of a special cargo at the port which had to be unloaded directly into inland craft. This queue in 1905 is at Woodside Flour Mill at Elland, West Yorkshire, on the Calder and Hebble Canal. This cargo of grain could have come either from Manchester docks or Hull docks. The boatwoman on one of the boats has taken the opportunity to do her washing, which can be done only when the boat is stationary.*

94. *The flexibility of road transport was the prinicipal reason for the downward trend in canal traffic after the First World War. Once motor lorries became reliable and could carry a reasonable payload they became a real threat. The forward-looking Grand Union Canal Company in 1937 operated a fleet of their own lorries to bring cargoes to the canal, and in turn to deliver them to the final customer. They even had a small fleet of sea-going vessels to bring caroges to Britain. The Second World War killed off this initiative but even so it is doubtful if the Grand Union Canal Company could have remained a viable trading unit.*

6. The people

Who were the boatmen who ran the boats on the British canal system? Some of the first boats trading on the Bridgewater Canal were probably estuarial craft and so the crews would have come from the estuary too, but when the narrow canals were opened there is little evidence that many working boatmen came from this source. Very few of the technical terms used on canal boats bear any resemblance to seafaring or coastal water terms. It can therefore be assumed that the first narrow boatmen came from the bank. The travelling life must have attracted gypsies, who were used to keeping and using horses, but canal boatmen in recent years have hated the term 'water gypsy'. Other boatmen could have been the local carriers, possibly driven out of a job by the canal, farm labourers and even former canal navvies. Gradually this assortment of people blended themselves into a boating community.

At first the boats were very plain and as many of the journeys were short the boats did not have cabins. Those that did were almost exclusively crewed by men. With the coming of competition from the railways, it became necessary for whole families to run the boats to cut down the costs. There was now the woman's influence in the cabins and in the decoration. By this time the company boats had different liveries, and the 'number ones' vied with each other over the decoration of their boats. It is not known where the traditional roses and castles decoration comes from, though similar motifs are found in the Balkans. It probably has its origins in the boatmen's background, perhaps from the gypsies or even the fairground.

The boatman's cabin was approximately 10 feet (3 metres) long by 6 feet 8 inches (2 metres) wide, and in this space large families lived and grew up. George Smith, a fervent social reformer of the mid nineteenth century, campaigned for laws which restricted the number of people who could live in each cabin. In response to this, the boatmen often built a small cabin in the bow of the boat for the children to sleep in. Most boatmen's children did not go to school, but with the coming of stricter educational laws they were encouraged to go to a local school whenever the boat was stationary, loading or unloading. The Grand Union Canal Company in the 1930s ran a floating school at Bulls Bridge, Southall in London.

Life for the boatmen was very hard. Most of them were paid by

95. As boatmen were always on the move, it was unusual to get a photograph of a large number of crew from one carrying company together. This photograph was taken at Braunston, Northamptonshire, when the boatmen were on strike in 1923, one of the few occasions when there had been a strike on the canal system. Note the varied styles of dress.

96. A canal painter at work on decorative water cans. Some boatmen decorated their own cans but most relied on the painter from the boatyard. These cans were the boatman's only means of storing drinking water. They were kept on the cabin roof and often chained down, as in this photograph taken after the Second World War, to stop them being brushed off the roof by overhanging branches.

97 (above). *Between the locks at Welsh Frankton in Shropshire on the Montgomeryshire Canal was a small boatbuilding yard at one time owned by John Beech. A number of individual traders used this yard, including S. Owen of Pant near Llanymynech. John Beech, who has just finished painting this boat, is standing in the cabin doorway. Such was the state of business that John Beech also traded with a couple of boats of his own.*

98 (opposite, top). *Children were often dressed as smaller versions of their parents, particularly the girls. This charming study shows the boat 'Tamara' belonging to Joseph Phipkin, a trader on the Grand Junction Canal. Young children were a problem, and accidents and drownings were not uncommon. Often children were tied to the cabin tops to prevent them falling off.*

99 (opposite, bottom). *A boatmen's christening party in 1913. Bonnets were a popular head-dress in the 1880s and 1890s but usually they were light in colour. With the death of Queen Victoria in 1901 even the boat people went into mourning and the women quickly acquired black bonnets. Many of them continued to wear black well into the 1920s and even the 1930s. This is Long Buckby on the Grand Junction Canal during a stoppage for repairs.*

results, so it was in their interests to get cargoes to their destination as quickly as they could. Most would work from dawn till dusk, often later in winter. At many of the wharves they would have to load and unload the boat themselves. Any delay at the wharfside or due to a canal stoppage would mean a loss of earnings. So keen were they to get on that there were often fights about whose right it was to use a lock when boats approached from opposite directions. At nights boatmen preferred to moor at a public house. Visiting a pub was one of their few forms of relaxation and accordion music was one of their few entertainments. Many pubs also had stables for the boat horses. The boatmen bought food when and wherever they could. A hold-up at a flight of locks might give them the opportunity to visit a

100. *Fellows, Morton and Clayton supplied a uniform to their crew. They wore corduroy trousers, either brown or white, a wide leather belt, metal-buttoned waistcoat, a jacket and a hat. It was hot work down in the enclosed boiler room of the steamers, so it is not surprising that some of the clothing has been discarded in this view. The butty 'Oak' behind has a bow cabin for the boatmen's children.*

101. *The boatmen on the wider Leeds and Liverpool Canal were little different from their narrowboat colleagues. Strong corduroy trousers, wide belt and braces were all similar. The clutter is unusual and shows the boat to be moored up. The little painted box on the right by the dog is a ventilator cover for the cabin below. The horse's feeding tin is on the stool on the left and behind it are the drinking-water barrel and dog kennel.*

nearby village store. On some of the trunk routes there would be a few food shops especially for the boatmen. Blacksmiths were needed at regular intervals, as were cobblers and shops which sold items such as cans for drinking water and ropes. The boatmen also lived off the land; poaching was commonplace and the boater's dog had to earn its keep.

Ceremonies such as christenings, weddings and funerals were important occasions in the lives of the boatmen. Christenings and weddings were joyful family gatherings, when everyone wore their best clothes, and after the service there would be a party at the canalside pub with plenty of music and merriment. Most boatmen regarded a particular town as their home, even though they had no house or family there. It may just have been the place

102. The canalside boatyard was very much part of the boatman's life. Most years his boat would be 'docked' for a check-up and essential repairs. Usually the boat would be taken into dry dock, and often this was the only opportunity the boatman had for taking a holiday. One of the most famous yards was that of Tooley Brothers of Banbury. Here they are seen caulking the seams of a wooden boat in 1940.

103. *The narrowboat family scene changed very little after the Second World War. This family seen at Hawkesbury Junction, Warwickshire, is awaiting orders for the next cargo of coal. This is a pair of Samuel Barlow boats, whose home base was Nursers Yard at Braunston, where they would have been decorated. The anchor symbol beside the rudder was their trademark. It was unusual for the paintwork to weather in this way.*

104. *Life for the boatwomen was hard. Not only did they help run the boats, steer and operate locks but they also had a 'home' to run. They had to cook meals, often from a pot simmering all day on the cabin range. Shopping had to be done, perhaps on a snatched visit to a canalside village store, and everything had to be planned so as to keep the boat on the move. Washing of clothes was a problem and only possible when the boats were moored up. Here the washing was done in a tub which takes the form of an old barrel. The mangle would have been carried on the boat, often getting in the way of the cargo.*

105 and 106. *The Grand Union Canal Company, in an attempt to make life easier for boatmen trading over their waters, opened a school for boat children at Bulls Bridge, South-all. It was dedicated by the Bishop of Bermuda in September 1930. The school was in the converted wideboat 'Elsdale', which was at first floating at the canalside. In 1939 the hull became unserviceable and the boat was pulled up on to the bank but continued to be used as before. These photographs were taken around 1940. The school closed in the late 1950s.*

they were born. When a boatman died, his body was often taken back by boat (travelling fly, through day and night) to his home town.

Some people thought that the canal boatmen lived less than blameless lives and missions were set up for them. The London City Mission, which had a hall at Brentford especially for the boating community, was the most famous and lasted until well after the Second World War. The Salvation Army also took an interest in their welfare.

During the Second World War a number of boatmen were called up to serve in the forces, whilst for others boating was a reserved occupation. Traffic on the canals increased and new boatmen were recruited. Several crews of women were trained by Kit Gayford and worked on the Grand Union Canal. Many other categories of people who worked on the canals have already been mentioned: lock-keepers, lengthmen, maintenance crews and so

107. *Decorating a boat with holly and ivy was not a common practice, but it is assumed that this photograph was taken at Christmas time, most probably in the 1920s. The look of the clothes gives some idea of the hard life of the boat crews. The young child is partially hidden behind the girl on the left and is clutching a toy animal.*

108. *At many of the principal stopping places on the canal there were boatmen's chapels. A narrowboatman would often drop in for a chat and a cup of tea, especially to those run by the Salvation Army. At Brentford the London City Mission had a presence well into the post-war years. In this photograph taken in 1924, Richard Knight, the missionary, is dressed as Father Christmas and has brought his own good fairy, his granddaughter Gladys Worseley, with him. There were few toys on a narrowboat, and Christmas presents such as these would have been most welcome.*

109. *During the Second World War the Grand Union Canal Company recruited girl volunteers to run some of its boats. In this photograph two trainees are seen on the motorboat on the right whilst the steerer of the butty unseen in the foreground was Eily 'Kit' Gayford, who trained many of these ladies. The tow-rope from the motorboat goes through running blocks on the butty to a stud mounted immediately in front of the steerer. In this way the butty steerer can control the length of the tow.*

110 (above). *On the canals there were lock-keepers only where there was a flight of locks. On rivers it was usual to have one keeper for each lock. Pretty Lincombe Lock, just outside Stourport in Hereford and Worcester, is now the northernmost lock on the river Severn. There was once a hermitage in the caves in the sandstone outcrop in the background. The lock-keeper and his assistant on the left are seen here in 1904. The gas lamp is a reminder that there was still night traffic on the river.*

111 (opposite). *The canals are used by many people, some of whom are not connected with the commercial traffic. The towpath was often a local right of way and the quickest way between two points was often 'along the cut'. Fishing has always been a popular sport and this 1910 scene at Blaby in Leicestershire shows some enthusiasts and some amateur fishermen.*

on. They all led relatively ordinary lives 'on the bank' and they lived in houses, so they did not form such tightly knit communities as the boatmen. Some changed over to become boatmen, usually as a result of marriage. Some boatwomen married land folk and left the boats.

As the canals declined the boatmen had to seek a living in a more conventional way. Some changed voluntarily or were tempted by much higher wages in factories. They even got used to living in a house. A few of the celebrities, such as Jo Skinner, Chocolate Charlie Atkins and Arthur Bray, lived on in the cabins of their boats.

Although working boatmen have disappeared, the land-based teams are still at work keeping the canals open for pleasure boats.

7. Postscript

This book has traced in words and pictures the coming of the canals to Britain. It has explained how they operated and described the boats and people that used them. It has given examples of how some of the canals declined and were closed.

In 1948 the canals were nationalised and the major fleets were combined under British Waterways. There was an improvement in the maintenance of both craft and waterways and working conditions and pay were improved. The severe winter of 1962-3 might have brought carrying to an end because the cut was iced up for months but the toll system was abolished and boats paid a licence fee instead, like cars. This allowed a number of new operators to start up and keep carrying going. Long-haul canal carrying ceased in 1972. Since the Second World War, however, there has been great interest in the leisure use of the waterways, particularly cruising. Many canals are now busier with hire boats and cruising craft than they were with commercial traffic in the heyday of the Victorian period. British Waterways, whilst still underfinanced, is able to keep the major canals open and enthusiasts spend thousands of hours restoring disused canals so that they too can join the cruising network. The future of the canals is assured.

86

Further reading

Burton, Anthony. *The Canal Builder*. Eyre Methuen, 1972.
Chaplin, Tom. *The Narrow Boat Book*. Whitter Books, 1978.
Hadfield, Charles. Various titles on individual canals ('The Canal Series'). David and Charles.
Hanson, Harry. *The Canal Boatmen*. Manchester University Press, 1975.
Lewery, Tony. *Narrow Boat Painting*. David and Charles, 1974.
Paget-Tomlinson, Edward W. *The Complete Book of Canal and River Navigations*. Waine Research Publications, 1978.
Rolt, L. T. C. *Inland Waterways of England*. George Allen and Unwin, 1950 and later impressions.
Ware, Michael E. *Narrow Boats at Work*. Moorland Publishing, 1980.

112. *Although the last traditional long-haul traffic of coal ceased in 1972, one short-haul run continued until 1981. This was the 'lime juice run' from Brentford in London to Boxmoor in Hertfordshire up the Grand Union Canal. Casks of lime pulp from Dominica and the Gold Coast came into the Royal Docks (later Tilbury) and were carried by lighter to Brentford, where they were stored in a British Waterways warehouse until required. British Waterways kept the boats going on this, their last contract, until April 1973, but because of lack of maintenance on the boats they had to give it up. It was taken on by independent carriers, who continued running two or three boats a week from September to April until October 1981. The traffic ceased then only because Cadbury Schweppes, owner of Rose's Lime Juice, chose to move manufacturing to a factory away from the canal. The pulp now comes in by road. In this photograph in British Waterways days the former Grand Union Canal Carrying Company motor boat 'Bargus' is being unloaded at Boxmoor Wharf.*

Places to visit

Intending visitors are advised to find out the opening times before making a special journey.

Black Country Museum, Tipton Road, Dudley, West Midlands DY1 4SQ. Telephone: 021-557 9643 or 9644.

Boat Museum, The National Waterways Museum, Dockyard Road, Ellesmere Port, Cheshire L65 4EF. Telephone: 051-355 5017.

Canal Museum, Canal Street, Nottingham. Telephone: Nottingham (0602) 598835.

Clock Warehouse Canal Exhibition, London Road, Shardlow, Derby. Telephone: Derby (0332) 792844.

Linlithgow Union Canal Society Museum, Manse Road Basin, Linlithgow, West Lothian. Telephone: Linlithgow (0506) 844730.

Llangollen Canal Exhibition, The Wharf, Llangollen, Clwyd. Telephone: Llangollen (0978) 860702.

Waterways Museum, Stoke Bruerne, near Towcester, Northamptonshire NN12 7SE. Telephone: Northampton (0604) 862229.

ACKNOWLEDGEMENTS

The author wishes to acknowledge the help of the staff of the Waterways Museum, Stoke Bruerne. Photographs are acknowledged to: Ike Argent, 95; Cadbury Schweppes, 112; Fred H. Done, title page and 7, 16, 63, 67; the Francis Frith Collection, 4; Eily 'Kit' Gayford, 109; W. E. R. Hallgarth, 1; Hampshire County Museums Service, 31; H. G. W. Household, 15; Denys Hutchings, 84; Imperial War Museum, 18, 48, 105, 106; Kodak Museum, 36; Manchester Ship Canal Company, 6, 8, 12, 38; Museum of English Rural Life, 96; National Coal Board, 57; National Monuments Record, 2, 14; National Railway Museum, 13, 20, 30, 51, 77, 83; M. Palmer, 50; L. T. C. Rolt Archive, 9, 10, 26, 37, 78, 102; K. C. Ward, 101, 107, 108; Wat(ays Museum, 17, 24, 39, 41, 42, 43, 47, 61, 62, 85, 86, 89, 92, 9ం, 99, 100, 104; Wiltshire Library and Museum Service, 52. All other photographs, including the front cover, are from the author's collection.

88

Index

Numbers in italic refer to illustration numbers.